THE DRAGON WAY:

OPENING THE DOOR
TO SPIRITUAL MASTERY

BOOK I – THE PREPARATION

Jean Eilerman and Christin Kostoff

Booklocker.com, Inc.
2009

Dedication

We honor the Dragons, great Spiritual Masters that they are, especially Belleroux, Jocasta, and Fenton who have been working with us to bring their teachings to the world

We also honor Kwan-Yin, the great Dragon-Rider, whose statue has been moving on its own since the time the book started!

We are grateful for the assistance of St. Germain, Master of the 7th Violet Ray.

We thank Marie Diamond who originally mentioned the Dragon work to us.

We thank all students of the Dragons-past, present and to come- who courageously answered the call to awaken and to become Dragon-Riders.

And, finally, we dedicate this book to the ascension of all beings, as well as to the ascension of our beautiful "Garden Planet."

CONTENTS

Preface

This book began several years ago when a spiritual teacher told us of a past life of ours when we had studied Dragons and corresponded about them. After that, we began connecting with the Dragons in meditation, and this book began to take form. The Dragons began by giving us eight Wisdom-Keys that can help to dispel the illusions that keep us trapped in our egos and personalities. Gradually, the Dragons gave us more information and experiential exercises which help to integrate this information into our daily lives. At the core of the Dragon teachings is respect for matter and embodied life which has often been devalued in religious traditions. The Dragons stress that spiritual knowledge must not be accepted unless it meets the test of real lived-experience.

The title of this book, The Dragon Way, represents one of many paths to enlightenment. This particular path emphasizes the sacredness of embodiment and the recognition that matter and Spirit are the same, just different forms of the same Reality. This path also reveals the illusions that have imprisoned us all and reveals how we can break free of their influence.

The Dragons told us that they are Spiritual Masters who, like the Angels, were given a specific mission. Their mission has to do with energy. They know about embodied energy and that the destiny of all energy is to awaken to reach its goal, union with the Divine or Enlightenment. They are aware that *all* forms of creation are energy that move toward awakening. Once the energy of any form of creation is awakened, it begins to move in its naturally and Divinely-ordained path.

The pattern that energy takes in the embodied universe resembles the physical form of the Dragon (and its related forms of serpent and snake.) That pattern is a serpentine/spiral one. If we look at the cosmos with its spiral galaxies or at the shape of the brain, we see the pattern clearly.

The spiral pattern of energy also represents the cyclical nature of embodied life. For example, the cycle of life in the universe involves birth, maturity, death, new life. We also live *in* the spiral cycles of nature like night and day or the changing of the seasons.

The Dragons are eminently suited to teach us about this path to enlightenment because they *are* the Masters of the embodied energy that we are.

When we look back through history, we see that all early cultures throughout the world made reference to Dragons and respected their power and place. However, in the West, Dragons were spoken of as fantasy creatures who represented evil. This was because Dragons taught about embodied life and stressed inner wisdom and the sacredness of creation. These were arenas that the patriarchy associated with the "feminine." When these "feminine" teachings and beliefs began to threaten the patriarchal structures and authority, persecution began. "Feminine" power and knowledge, and all things associated with them, were labeled as evil and oppressed.

As a result of centuries of this thinking and practice by civil and ecclesiastical authorities, humans lost contact with the truth of Dragons. They also lost contact with the Dragons' connection with the Divine and with energy itself. Consequently, *we* lost contact with the truth of *our* heritage, a Divine heritage.

Humans forgot that they are Divine energy, embodied in form, moving through processes of initiation that would direct and purify the energy that they are and send them into their natural journey to re-unite with the Divine. Enter the Dragons ...

The time is right to remember our heritage. The time is now to act on this information. The entire universe is conspiring to raise the level of consciousness on Earth and for all beings that inhabit Earth.

Enlightenment—being the light that we are-- is our birthright. It is what we were born for. The Dragons are here to shout out that truth to all who are willing to listen. The Dragons are here to help us remember who we really are and, as we remember, we help the rest of our earthly companions to remember that we are all of God. We are all one, and we are all on our way Home into the full experience of this oneness.

The Dragons are also here to teach us that matter and Spirit are energy vibrating at different rates. All creation is made up of this sacred energy, waiting to awaken and move. Energy in its earth-form has been known by terms like "ley lines" or "vortexes". The energy in humans has been frequently spoken of in terms of "chakra centers," which are human "ley lines" and "vortices." The energy that we *are* is embedded in the bodily form and wrapped around the base of the spine. This resembles a coiled serpent/Dragon and has been called "kundalini" by the Hindu tradition. Thus, to move into enlightenment, one must stimulate and awaken the coiled energy and allow it to travel up to the crown of the head and beyond. The Dragons assist us to clear our energy centers so that the energy can move upward to trigger the opening of our consciousness which leads Homeward. (The illusions that the

Dragons point out in Book I restrict our energy and can prevent the upward movement.)

The Dragons, then, are Masters of embodied energy who bring the fire of their alchemy to assist us to move through all barriers and to allow the natural process of our remembrance and transformation to occur.

So, seemingly disparate areas like the "feminine," Dragons, embodiment, kundalini, and enlightenment are actually all related. Because this is the time that supports energy moving into higher levels of vibration (consciousness growth), all the seeming dualities and apparent contradictions are at last coming together into a whole picture.

Book I: The Preparation begins the process by focusing on certain Wisdom-Keys. Aligning with these keys is essential in trying to clarify and clear the energy vessels that we are. This is the foundation upon which we can build empowerment and transformation.

The information dealt with in this book, and those to come, works hand in hand with the Dragon Mystery School. The Mystery School is an ancient form known as a "university of the soul." The Dragon Mystery School is offered in the San Francisco Bay area and by teleconference to those living across the world.

There will be four levels of the Mystery School. These levels focus on *experiencing* the alchemy that the Dragons bring, an alchemy whose goal is becoming the Divine beings that we are and restoring all creation to this Truth.

We invite you to go to the website www.dragonmysteryschool.com and read more.

The chapters of Book 1 will present activities and assignments. These are the ways to make the information presented here come alive in you. It's not about just reading words and ideas, but about inviting the spark that sits within you to *grow* and *glow* and *fire* and *burst into flame and light*! This is the *true key*. That which is given is a catalyst that has the power to ignite you and to ignite the world!

One of the most important tools to assist in the igniting of your inner fire is a consistent meditation practice. There are many forms of meditation, and it is important to choose one which helps to clear and protect the personality field, as well as one which helps to align your personality with your soul and your I Am Presence. (See Appendix 4)

Jean Eilerman and Chris Kostoff
October 2008
Santa Rosa, California

P. S. If you are attracted to the Dragon work, whether it be reading the book, taking the classes, or both, know that by holding the intention to experience the Dragon knowledge and to move on to your path to enlightenment, you are calling upon powerful spiritual beings who will begin to interact with you.

Don't be surprised if Dragons "fly into your life" in varied and unusual forms!

If, after reading this book and doing some of the exercises, you have questions about changes that you observe in your life, please e-mail us:

jean@dragonmysteryschool.com
chris@dragonmysteryschool.com

Introduction

In the recent film, *Eragon*, based on the book of the same name, it was said, "The time of the Dragon-Riders will come again." The time of the Dragons, as well as the time of the Dragon -Riders, is here *now*.

Once upon a time, we were taught that Dragons existed only in fairy tales and in children's imaginations. Yet, how do we explain the fact that Dragons have appeared in stories and myths in all parts of the world and in every culture? Could these stories and myths represent an old wisdom, an old experience that the human race lived in the distant past?

In the West, Dragons were described negatively as mythical evil creatures that hoarded treasure, kidnapped princesses, and burned and pillaged the countryside. In the East, however, Dragons were portrayed positively as Gods or messengers from the Gods who actively were involved with human life. Even today, the Dragon occupies a special role in Eastern life, not only as a symbol of the Emperor and royal households, but the Dragons are important central forces in the world of Feng Shui.

What is the truth about Dragons?

Dragons are real and have lived on earth. Their influence on humankind is real. Dragons are Spiritual Masters, somewhat like angels.

The mission of the Dragons is to empower and transform. In the pages that follow, the Dragons will share their Wisdom-Keys with us. They are the *real life coaches* who bring us the possibility of our empowerment if we live in truth.

The essence of the Dragons' wisdom teaches us about the world of illusions and about the true nature of embodiment.

The World of Illusions: We have been breathing in and creating illusions since we first populated this planet. After so long, it is difficult to even see where the truth lies. As we look at our planet today, we see the results of living these illusions: people feel worthless and disconnected, wars and injustice are rampant, and the environment is suffering. What are the illusions that create these conditions, and how do we pull ourselves out of this mess? The Dragons' Wisdom-Keys will help us. Now, more than ever, we need the Dragons and their fire-breath to burn away the false beliefs we so easily accept and respond to. Now, more than ever, we need to re-find truth and to rebuild our lives around what counts and what opens us up to real fulfillment. Dragons burn the illusions that constrict us and lie to us.

The True Nature of Embodiment: The major illusion that we have lived with is that matter and Spirit are two separate realities. This illusion has caused centuries of pain! When we live this illusion, we tend to either throw ourselves into a life of material pleasure and possessions or try to remain pure by rejecting the material world and its "temptations." Both of these ways have been wrong.

The Dragons are here with the truth. **It is all Spirit.**

Just as water, ice, and steam can appear to be different substances, they are in fact the same thing under differing conditions. Steam is not more "holy" or "elevated" than water or ice; it is just a different form. But the form needs to be respected. Matter has been disrespected because it has limits and appears to be different from limitless Spirit. We have been told that these limits are present due to the original sin of mankind. This is a lie!

Matter is not bad or opposed to Spirit. It is a manifestation of Spirit that has its own set of limits and rules. For example, matter tends to age; matter has dimensions like weight and is time-bound and space-bound. When we respect matter, we understand that matter has its separate set of rules but is not less than that which is Spirit. It is Spirit in another form.

The Dragons are here now to assist us to live fully as embodied ones and to love the embodied as expressions of the Divine.

Wisdom-Key #1: The Truth of Creation

There is a Grand Plan for all creation, and it includes you.

The Illusion We Live With

Modern life seems out of control and chaotic, senseless, brutal, selfish, lacking honor and purpose. Stories abound of genocide, starvation, the rich and powerful hurting the innocent, depression, suicides and domestic abuse. There appears to be no order, no plan, no justice, and evil seems to be winning. When you experience this every day, you believe the illusion that creation has no meaning, no order, no plan, no direction, and that there is no ultimate goal to life.

How This Illusion Impacts Society and the World

When you are stuck in this illusion, the pain and loss that you see around you and that you suffer yourselves seem like a punishment rather than a tool for your growth. This effects how you treat others and yourselves. You often see others and yourselves as victims. When you see yourselves as victims, you are less able to spring back into life from the losses you experience. And, you can project your anger, blame, and guilt onto other individuals, cultures and nations.

When you view life as having a greater purpose, you don't get stuck in the misfortunes that befall humans as a regular part of living. You realize that your pain and losses are part of a bigger picture and vision. Everything happens for a reason, even when you are not aware of what that reason is.

The Dragons' Fire Message

Dear Ones, we breathe on you now with an urgency that has not ever been seen. Our breath awakens you to the truth and to your role in the evolving plan of the One. You have slept long enough, and it is the time of the great awakening. Creation is moving forward, and you are to take your place. We return now into consciousness to stimulate you and the Earth as the energy channels of the One that you are. Remembrance and action are called for now. Wherever you are in your life's journey, it is time to realize what centuries of illusions have disguised and tried to keep hidden. We are with you. We breathe over you. We call you. Listen, feel and allow the sleeping Dragon that you are to fully awaken and to fully emerge. We are a team together, moving Homeward.

Realigning with Wisdom-Key #1: The Truth of Creation

There is a Grand Plan.

Everything that happens is part of this plan.

The Dragons are here at this time to help you see the Homeward path. They are here to tell you once again that creation has a meaning, has a direction, and that direction is toward wholeness and union with all that is. You matter. Your choices matter. Even though you are moving towards union with God, your choices will determine how smooth or rough your path to God is and how long it may take. As you open your consciousness and clear your energy, your movement is accelerated, and your choices become clearer. You came from the Source and are returning to that Source. This has been known by the Dragons from the beginning. It is time for *you* to remember.

Because you do not believe in the Grand Plan, you have fallen into despair and loneliness and have lost your integrity and values. When you believe in the Grand Plan, you believe that there is a higher purpose, even when misfortunes occur in your lives. You see that life has a natural rhythm of good and bad situations and experiences, and you don't take personally the traumatic events of life and judge and condemn yourself as dumb or deserving of punishment.

Whatever experiences you have, it doesn't change the fact that your essence is of the Divine. Difficult and challenging situations are a part of the rules of embodiment. They are how you learn the lessons that you need for your journey. What a difference it would make if you truly believed that everything that happens in your lives forwards the Divine Plan. It helps you to make lemonade from lemons. Even when bad things happen, they will eventually have a positive effect on your lives.

Consider the old Chinese legend where a farmer buys a horse. The horse no sooner arrives than he runs away. "Oh, no," says the farmer, "What will I do? I have no transportation!" He decides to send his only son to look for the horse. In the process of finding the horse, the son breaks his leg and is immobilized. "Oh no," says the farmer, "I have no help on my farm. What will I do?" Then, the king's men arrive to round up young men for war. The son can't be conscripted since he has broken his leg.

If you stop at any one point of the story, you fail to *get* the importance of the final event. If you look carefully back into

7

your lives, can't you find similar tales and events? Don't they point you to seeing that there is a grand design?

When you view life from the limited perspective of your personality, it is difficult to see the entire picture with its broader implications. It is rather like looking at a room through a keyhole as opposed to opening the door and seeing the entire scene. When your view is expanded, you see how all the parts of the Plan fit together. Sometimes you are not able to see how all the parts do fit and must trust in the Divine Plan.

Meditation for Wisdom-Key #1

We Dragons would like to assist you in dissolving your illusions and remembering the truth. To do this, we ask to guide you in meditations to experience, in new ways, the truths we bring you.

So let us begin. Find a quiet place where you can spend some time by yourself.

Take a few breaths, clear your mind, and let it begin to wander. Call the Dragons to you. What do you see? What do you feel? What do you smell? Does one Dragon in particular come forward and catch your attention? What color is the Dragon? Is it male or female, how large, how many toes on its feet, how long is the tail? Will the Dragon talk to you if you ask him/her a question? Tell the Dragon that you are reading about his/her principles and wisdom-keys. Remember that Dragons may need several visits with you before they accept your sincerity. It may take a few tries before your Dragon is ready to connect with you.

With the Dragon's permission, climb on the Dragon's back and ask to go for a ride. Ask to be taken on a flight high into the sky where you can get a broader view and where you can see for miles. Perhaps you can see the Earth spinning in space. Flying gives you perspective. With this perspective, you begin to see order in what previously looked like chaos.

Ask your Dragon to take you back into a time in your life when a broader view would have helped you to see order and growth in a situation where you felt stuck, confused, and uncomfortable. What scene comes forward? Where are you in the scene? What others are present? With the help of your Dragon guide, step back from the emotions of the scene. As you see the big picture, you discover that all your experiences are connected and can bring lessons and skills that help you on your journey home. Every experience, whether you label it positive or negative, is a step on the path Homeward. What did you learn from this scene that can help you in other situations in your life?

Take some quiet time reflecting on all this. Then, when you are ready, ask the Dragon to take you back to your quiet place from where you began this ride.

Ask your Dragon to gently breathe its fire-breath over you to help in igniting your own fire. Dragons are known for breathing fire. When Dragons breathed fire over the earth, it was to clear illusions, especially the illusion that matter and Spirit are separate realities. You have your own fire-breath, and it is part of the human energy system. Human fire-breath comes from the unity of your intention and the actions that result.

Take as long as you wish absorbing and activating this principle in your body, in your consciousness, and in your life. Dragons are patient and gentle and do not want you to go forward until you are ready. Each principle is meant to bring truth and joy into your understanding of how important your life is to the full unfolding of the Divine Plan.

Tools for Integration of Wisdom-Key #1

1. *Affirmations/Positive Self-Messages*--Repeat two times per day for two weeks:

    a. There is a Grand Plan that guides the universe and all life.

    b. All of creation is interconnected and comes from the one Source.

    c. I change my life by living the Dragons' wisdom which aligns me with the truth.

    d. When I unify my intention and will, it activates my inner fire.

2. *Journaling*—Take some quiet time and write from your own life experiences:

    a. Journal about negative life experiences that have later been seen to lead to positive outcomes. How does this change your view of the meaning of life?

3. *Other Activities*—These are different ways to integrate this Wisdom-Key:

    a. Read books that discuss the oneness of creation, e.g., books about Native American spirituality, Buddhism, Hinduism, yoga and meditation.

    b. Meditate daily, inviting your Dragon to be with you, becoming more acquainted with each other. Meditating daily is essential to protect your energy field and to learn to connect your personality, soul and I Am Presence. (See Appendix 4) If you do not have a daily meditation practice, we recommend that you find one or consider attending the Dragon Mystery School.

c. See if you can discover patterns in nature that indicate the order in creation, e.g., leaf patterns, snowflake patterns, cycles of life, and planetary designs. You might want to read books by Fritz Capra, David Boehm, Deepak Chopra, or Dr. Emoto.

d. Notice how the media focuses only on present negative situations, and you never see the positive outcomes that may take place later. Watch this.

Wisdom-Key #2: Honor Yourself and All Creation

*All creation comes from the Source. Remember to honor
yourself as part of the Source.*

The Illusion We Live With

Since there is no Grand Plan or direction for the world,
you have no vision for yourselves. Your lives and your actions
feel unimportant. You are like a ship without a rudder, an
anchor, or a home port. You feel tossed about by the winds of
chance and feel powerless. You feel alone and unsupported.
You experience no connecting links to Mother Earth or to other
forms of life.

How This Illusion Impacts Society and the World

When you don't honor yourselves, you certainly don't
honor others or Mother Earth. Some religious traditions teach
that you are sinners at birth. If you see yourselves and others as
sinners, then self-abuse and abuse of others becomes easy. You
fill your minds and bodies with unhealthy ideas, images, and
beliefs. Your personal relationships and communities are
poisoned by disregarding and disrespecting your families,
friends, and neighbors. You suspect anyone who is different,
especially different nations and ethnic and cultural groups. You
don't see differences as positive and enriching, but as a threat.
You pollute and rape Mother Earth who gave you life. All of
these actions are rooted in not honoring the self. The less you
honor yourselves, the less all beings are honored. This includes
Mother Earth!

The Dragons' Fire Message

Dear Ones, we invite you to awaken to the truth of your intended place in the Great Plan of creation. You are being called now to recognize your importance and to honor your place in the whole. Self-love or self-honoring is the very foundation that you can build on. It is like a spotlight shining on illusions. It clears your channels and produces an environment for the other Wisdom-Keys to grow and flourish. These Wisdom-Keys, rooted in self-love, change the lead of life into gold. When you put self-love into blocked channels, it begins the process of cleaning out. It is like a blocked drain. You put the drain cleaner, self-love, into the drain, and it percolates and begins the process of opening up and clearing out.

When you decide you want to change, open up, or become more *you*, you hold that intention for change. Then, you choose tools to manifest your intention. One of the tools is our Wisdom-Keys. Your intention and the use of the tool begin the internal process. The internal process, once begun, is not so much under your conscious control. Your own true nature guides the process. Trust us and trust yourself.

As the process deepens in you, you begin to really know that all creation is the *One in form.*

Remembering these three basic teachings will help you to really honor yourselves and all creation: I am not an accident; I am a child of the Divine, as is all of creation; and the Divine calls me to take my place in the Plan by honoring my individuality. We ask you to speak aloud and to write these teachings. Do this two times per day for nine days. At the end of nine days, call in your Dragon. Send these messages to the universe by calling in the Dragon-fire and burning the messages out in the sunshine. As your burn them, with your Dragon beside you, ask the universe to help in the integration and activation of these principles *in* you and *in* your life.

Realigning with Wisdom-Key #2: Honor Yourself and All Creation

I am not an accident.

I am a child of the Divine, as is all of creation,

The Divine calls me to take my place in the Plan by honoring my individuality

You *are* good enough. You *are* part of the Divine. It is time to see clearly and live out your role in the Plan. How would you act differently if you truly believed in your importance and in your value and in the value of each being around you? This is an important question that deserves your taking a little time to really ponder.

This is truly a revolutionary step and a step that has been talked about in many spiritual traditions. If you are to begin the journey Homeward, you must believe that it is *your* home and that *you* belong. You must begin to see who you are through your God-Eyes, the eyes that see your Divine nature as well as your material nature. You are not simply lumps of matter sent to live a lonely and separate existence. You are a strand of the web of life on planet Earth, and you share with that web of life a spark of the Divine that is in us all.

You were put here for a reason by your Source. You are valuable in and of yourselves. Whether you are nuclear scientists, the president of a country, or a garbage collector, you are playing out your role in the Plan. No role is insignificant. The wholeness of the Plan demands that you honor yourselves no matter what role you play.

The key to your happiness lies in acknowledging the truth of who you are and acting accordingly. Who you are is a connected being, connected to others and the Great Plan. Admit the truth and take your rightful place! Valuing yourselves as part of the Divine Plan is not a prideful act. **It is the truth**. Seeing this clearly evokes a new personal integrity, inspiring your self-love and self-trust and a valuing of all other beings as participants in the Plan. How this could change human history! Once you see the light in yourself, you see it in all others, including the Earth.

This principle of self-honoring tells you of your Divine as well as material nature, describes your essential part in the Divine Plan, and the value of each being in creation. As you integrate these truths, you feel that you belong, that you are not in competition with others, that your responsibility to the Plan is to fully cultivate who you are so that the Plan can fully blossom. You are left with the duty and the freedom to fully explore who you are, knowing you have a place in the whole, and you are not loved less because you are not rich and famous. As you do this, you begin to honor all beings and the Earth because you now value yourselves.

The teaching of "original sin" that told you of your sinful nature is false. The true "original sin" is *believing* this teaching. When you believe this, you believe that you are separated from God and other beings.

Meditation for Wisdom-Key #2

Sit in a quiet place. Take several deep breaths as you let go of outer distractions. Call in your special Dragon tour guide. When the Dragon arrives, imagine that you can place your hand on his/her face. Allow the Dragon to greet you. When you are ready, climb aboard the Dragon, who will slowly lift off the ground and out of this dimension.

The Dragon is taking you to a very special place: the chamber of mirrors. When you arrive there, you will see a huge, old wooden door. The Dragon will lead you through the door into a vast chamber where two giant mirrors sit. There may be many other things in the chamber to be discovered later, but for now he takes you to a seat before the mirrors.

The Dragon says: "Gaze into them. You will notice that they seem foggy and unclear."

Your Dragon touches one with its nose, and suddenly it clears. This mirror holds images of your life under the spell of the illusions about yourself. This is the mirror of the personality. Look deeply. Focus into the mirror and allow it to show you situations where false messages about yourself and the world have been presented. For example: "you are not good enough"; "you can't trust people who are different". See what some of these strong messages have been for you, their sources, and their repercussions.

Observe yourself under the influence of these illusions. How do you act and feel? Are you happy? Take as long as you need before this mirror.

When you are ready and have seen enough, ask your Dragon to move on. The Dragon touches the other mirror.

Your Dragon says: "Behold the mirror of your truth, the God-Eye Mirror. Look deeply and know." The new mirror clears gradually and lets in brilliant light. It may be hard to focus. Keep watching as the scene clears. Before you, you will see an image of yourself. The light seems to radiate from your face. Observe yourself closely. Surrounding you are many others, people of other races and nations, as well as animals and plants and rocks and stars. This is a picture where all creation is represented, and you are taking your rightful place. There is laughter. There are smiles. The tails of the animals are wagging. Longstanding enemies embrace before you. All those with whom you have differences and anger come to you and you embrace them. If you are unable to embrace all those that come, you may begin with a smile or a handshake.

The 'you' in the mirror is invited to speak about yourself, to tell the assembled who you are. Notice that as the image of you in the mirror speaks, all of the positive, true and beautiful words flow easily from you. You speak of your Divinity, your journey, your joy, your love, your mission and your place here on this planet. You smile; you breathe easily and deeply. Your eyes are bright, and peace fills the mirror.

As the scene grows quiet, your Dragon speaks. "Which of these do you choose for your life? Speak the choice clearly now for your life and the lives of others depend on it." This marks a beginning process of change into self-honoring. The

Dragon knows that you will need to look into these mirrors many times.

If you are ready to choose the last image, tell your Dragon now. If you are not ready at all, you may thank your Dragon, ask to go home, and you may return when you are ready. The Dragon will help you any time you ask.

If you are ready, and if you choose the true you, your Dragon will come close to the mirror of illusions. Your Dragon will first breathe deeply and send its fire-breath over the mirror. The mirror will shatter and vaporize. Then, your Dragon turns to *you*. He breathes the fire-breath over you. All the false illusions will be ignited in the fire. The illusions about yourself are burning up now. Ask the Dragon to take you home slowly. Take your time as you return to a sense of the outer world.

It's essential to rest today. Write your reflections. Know that the process of burning will continue as long as it needs. This is happening within you now. **It is real**. Freedom and release are in process within you. You will remember the true you, and he or she will emerge more fully into manifestation.

Tools for Integration of Wisdom-Key #2

1. *Affirmations/Positive Self-Messages*—Repeat two times per day for two weeks:

   a. I hold a valuable place in the Divine Plan along with all other aspects of creation.

   b. I am important and irreplaceable to the flowering of the Divine Plan.

   c. I recognize my value and uniqueness.

d. I recognize the value and uniqueness of all people.

e. I embrace myself and others with forgiveness, love and joy.

f. All of creation is sacred and shares the light of the Source.

g. I am one with all creation, one in our diversity.

h. The Earth herself is the Body of the Divine and I treat her as such.

i. I am never alone and always loved and supported by the Source.

2. *Journaling*—Take some quiet time and write from your own life experiences:

a. How do I honor myself, my friends and family, other cultures and people and Mother Earth?

b. How do I dishonor myself, my friends and family, other cultures and people and Mother Earth?

c. Do I compare myself with others? Do I judge myself? When I do this, how do I feel? How do I feel about the others that I compare myself with?

d. Do I believe that my life has purpose? What purpose?

e. Do I feel I contribute to life on this planet? Can the "average person" make a difference?

f. What is my view of those that differ from me?

g. Do I treat males and females with equal respect?

h. How does my behavior show my attitudes toward the rest of creation and the Earth herself?

3. *Other Activities*—These are different ways to integrate this Wisdom-Key:

   a. You may want to go on the internet using www.google.com or go to the library and survey information on the following topics:

      i. Co-dependency: Do you live your life through another rather than pursuing your own heart's desire?

      ii. Learned Helplessness: Have negative messages from others now become your messages to yourself?

      iii. Power of Positive Thinking and Self-Esteem: Can you achieve wondrous things if you believe in yourself? Explain.

      iv. Web of Life and Oneness of Creation: Can understanding your oneness with all help you to see the fullness of the Divine Plan and your part in it? How?

   b. Read newspapers and magazines, watch TV, go to the movies, listen to radio and find out how the illusions based on not honoring yourself are working in today's world.

Wisdom-Key #3: Commitment to the Truth

Integrating Wisdom-Keys 1 and 2 into your life requires commitment and commitment draws obstacles.

The Illusion We Live With

When you make a commitment, it is easy and can happen quickly. You only have to decide what commitment you want to make, and it will happen. No pain, upset or upheaval is necessary. When commitment brings obstacles with it, you can make another commitment and avoid the obstacles. After all, difficulties must mean your initial choice was the wrong choice.

Beware of commitments because they can be a drag. They can make you rigid, and you don't need an organizing principle to make your life meaningful.

How This Illusion Impacts Society and the World

If you believe the illusions about commitment, you are untrustworthy because you either don't make any commitments, or if you do, you don't honor your commitments. This is true whether you are an individual or a nation. In the past, it was said that "your word was your bond", meaning that, if you promised or pledged to do something, you did it, no matter how difficult or inconvenient it was. People were more able "back then" to trust and to base their decisions on your follow-through.

Making a commitment is often difficult, but once you make a commitment, it is necessary to keep it if at all possible because that act reflects on who you are as a person or a nation.

Because obstacles come up does not automatically mean that your commitment is wrong. Obstacles *will* come up, and they test the strength of your commitment.

How can the world function if nations do not keep their commitments in the forms of treaties and agreements? This would lead to chaos and *has* done so. What happens to nations and the world when they do not keep their commitment to their national ideals and identity? Why would other nations enter into agreements with them, support them, or partner with them in projects?

If you have no organizing principles either as an individual or a nation, you have no standards to base your actions on. Anything goes in your life, but there is no direction nor any means available to chart a direction. Where you go and what you do depends on your purpose. Without any guiding principle, you don't know what your purpose is and, therefore, can't plan sustained meaningful action.

How does a nation plan its agenda if it has no underlying philosophy to which it is committed? Even if greed or power is an underlying commitment, it gives a direction to action. Successful action needs a plan, and a plan proceeds from some kind of commitment. The absence of commitment results in meaningless, erratic action.

A realistic long term commitment takes into consideration that change does not progress in a straight line. There will be times of doubt, frustration, fear and impatience. Commitment to the goal carries you through these difficult times. The fable of the tortoise and the hare enables you to see that an effective commitment involves persistence and consistency. (The civil rights legislation of the 1960's has now given birth to an African-American U. S. President.)

The Dragons' Fire-Message

Dear Ones, can we count on you? This is the time when you need to show up and make a decision. There is no way around making this decision. You either make the commitment and move forward, or you cannot accept this gift of our teachings. For it is in the making of this commitment that our teachings will unfold in you.

We have given you the truth of who you are. You must now accept it or reject it. This invitation requires your response!

Realigning with Wisdom-Key #3: Commitment to the Truth

The first and second wisdom-keys require a shifting of your fundamental perspective of life. By accepting these principles, you have acknowledged the existence of the Divine Plan, your place in that Plan, and the journey of creation Homeward. When you base your actions on the existence of an ultimate goal, it influences your choices. When you believe that even obstacles and challenges can bring you closer to the ultimate goal, life is less fear-filled, and you feel stronger because you know you are part of a greater reality.

This ultimate commitment to Truth is one of the most important you will make, for it is a commitment to your **true selves** and your **destiny**. The commitment you are being asked to make based on the truths of the first two Wisdom-Keys, is a commitment your personality is making to align with the truth of your I AM PRESENCE. This commitment reflects a remembrance and an acknowledgement of your Divine nature as well as your material nature. **This is the pivotal commitment of your life**. It is about the very definition of **who**

you are! This commitment also brings a sense of direction to your lives and knowledge that everything you do matters.

This is the life-changing step. If you truly integrate this key, rather than just reading words, you will need to examine what fits in your life and what does not. Your lives will change.

To really believe that you matter in a world that devalues all but the rich and famous can be a shock to your system. Becoming empowered in this way is not easy and can bring up your old fears and inadequacies. To really believe that misfortune will offer you gifts is not to ignore that misfortune is hurtful, but this gives you a whole new way of seeing beyond the hurt.

Not only will this commitment bring up old fears and inadequacies, but obstacles will present themselves almost immediately. Dealing with obstacles is not only a way of learning needed lessons, but can serve to make the commitment stronger. Dealing successfully with obstacles enhances your self-confidence.

This commitment is freeing rather than limiting because you think and act as a whole being rather than a conflicted ego-bound collection of desires. With your energies in alignment, you are able to achieve more and experience more of what you desire, because there is a flow and direction of energy that is clear and unblocked. Your commitment to these principles also is marked by a belief in the oneness of creation and a respect for all as equal participants in the Plan.

This principle asks you to go beyond your comfort zones and to empower yourselves as God intended.

Real commitment can't be forced; it comes at a point of soul- readiness. Though there are things you can do to facilitate this commitment, the final act of total dedication and belief occurs in its own timing.

Meditation for Wisdom-Key # 3

Close your eyes. Breathe deeply and relax.

Your Dragon approaches you before you even call.

Your Dragon touches your face very sweetly and tells you that you are going to a special place, without the necessity of a flight. The Dragon breathes over you.

You get cozy and feel warm waves of breath envelop you.

You become aware that you and your Dragon are standing in a cave-like, ancient alchemical laboratory. The Dragon knows a great deal about alchemy, as Dragons are Master Alchemists and they have known many such beings throughout history.

You come into a room filled with smells and retorts, odd objects and vials. There may even be a faint mist hanging in the room.

The Dragon asks you to approach a table and sit before it. As you sit, the Dragon places before you containers, like test tubes, and a very special case containing secret ingredients.

The light grows dim in the rest of the cave-room, only illuminating the area before you.

Your Dragon asks you to choose a large test tube, and you place it in front of you. Then, with the Dragon's assistance, you are asked to hold the intention of breathing into this vessel your current life-force and energy. You lean close to the clear container and hold the intention: "I now breathe into this vessel an image of my current life force and energy so that I may see it clearly."

Then, you breathe over the container, and slowly you watch it fill.

The Dragon asks you to examine what you see…color, texture, images.

Then, the Dragon brings the case of secret ingredients close to you. The case is opened, and there are many vials to choose from, and two vials are selected. The vials are removed from the case, and you see that they are labeled.

You look closely and see that they are labeled as the first two wisdom-keys. The vials contain the energetic essence of these Truths.

The Dragon asks you to open both and, before you simultaneously pour drops of both into the vial of *your* energy, the Dragon asks you, "Do you choose to proceed now, even if you don't know all the changes that are to come?" If you are ready, then you open them, take them in your hands and pour drops from both. (If you are not ready, you ask your Dragon to take you home, and you can return when you desire.)

You replace the vials on the countertop, and the Dragon puts them away as you sit back to watch.

Your Dragon asks you to watch the vial of your life-force. "When the essence of these Truths enters the vial, what happens to *your essence*?" You try to hold onto some words of description to remember later.

When you integrate these Truths with your life energy, you are not the same as before. Your path has been cleared. You cannot return to unknowing. You cannot return to a place of not caring. You will continue to transform totally and to commit to whatever the *Truth of You is.*

Before you and your Dragon leave, your Dragon says: "Beloved, take these thoughts into your heart. Decide what is asked of you since you have been given these gifts. What choices do you need to make now as a result?"

Ponder these things deeply within you.

Tools for Integration of Wisdom-Key #3

1. *Affirmations/Positive Self-Messages*—Repeat two times per day for two weeks:

    a. When obstacles present themselves, I can calmly find new options to pursue.

    b. My commitment to my highest self and destiny is enhanced by my persistence and fidelity over time.

    c. My life is changing, and I will find the support I need to thrive with these changes.

    d. I have made the commitment to follow my path Home and to trust that my choices will bring me to the God in me.

    e. I have the courage and strength needed to remain clear and firm in all commitments.

2. *Journaling*—Take some quiet time and write from your own life experiences:

    a. Where do I find support to help me maintain my commitments?

b. My actions and choices are guided by my commitment to the truth of Wisdom-Keys 1 and 2. What changes does this make in my life? Areas to consider are: relationships with myself, family and friends, my career, how I spend my money, how I look at and participate in my community, my country and the world.

c. When I find areas of my life not in alignment with my commitment to the truth, what changes need to be made?

d. In the past, how did I establish my priorities? Did I have an overreaching principle or principles that I used when I had to make important decisions about career and relationships?

3. *Other Activities*—These are different ways to integrate this Wisdom-Key:

a. Anchoring the principle of commitment requires that you deepen an internal dialogue with your Higher Self. This is a time when your ego/personality more clearly aligns itself with the Higher Self and Wisdom-Keys 1 and 2. Meditation, quiet time alone and journaling will allow you to review your life and see what is in alignment or out of alignment with your journey Home. Give yourself the time and quiet necessary to strengthen your connection with and trust of the God in you.

b. Read about the lives of people who have truly allowed this commitment to activate their lives, people such as Gandhi, Mother Teresa, Martin

Luther King, Nelson Mandela, the Dali Lama and many others.

c. Look around you. Are there people and institutions that clearly operate on this principle of commitment?

Wisdom Key #4: The Principle of Action

Identify Your Goal. Take Action. Remain Flexible.

The Illusion We Live With

Making the commitment to Keys 1, 2 and 3 is really all I need to do. The universe will take care of the rest, and I won't have any problems. Action isn't important because I have made the spiritual commitment to my journey Home. If I do act in response to my commitment, the universe will insure that all will go forward smoothly according to my plan.

How This Illusion Impacts Society and the World

What happens to society when you fail to act; when you believe that the spiritual commitment you have made is all that is necessary? When you don't act, you disempower yourself, and nothing changes or happens. Spiritual commitment to the ultimate goal is necessary, but you also live in the physical world, and you must act in the physical world. Without any physical action, nothing will ever change. If a commitment is to be made real in the physical world, you must follow through with an action plan. How many commitments have you made in the past that went nowhere because you failed to act?

How does the world ever change if good intentions remain only in the mind? How often do governments pass environmental or social-change laws and then no money is appropriated to initiate action? **Nothing changes**. You condemn governments who practice genocide, but unless nations rise up and *do* something the genocide continues. **Nothing changes**.

There has been criticism of the United Nations because they have great discussions about world problems, but then **nothing happens**. Good people can make a difference, but it all depends on translating commitment into action.

The Dragons' Fire-Message

Beloved Ones, we support your taking action in the world to manifest your commitments. There will be moments when great courage and strength are called for because your actions, which are based on the Dragon Wisdom-Keys, fly in the face of current popular belief and practice. But, to know yourself and to make the Dragon principles and your commitment real, action *is* necessary.

Proper action demands flexibility and adaptability. They are gifts that help you to use the normal changes of life to move ahead. Recognizing the reality that obstacles will occur, will move you forward on your sacred path and will not allow obstacles to stop you.

When Dragons are ready to move, their fire clears the path. The Dragons don't hesitate once they begin. We set our goals, propose avenues of action and start. Once you really know you are part of the whole, with an assignment, there is no reason to linger. Goal setting is important because fire (energy) needs a target. Without a vision or plan, energy doesn't know where to go, and you burn yourselves up or out. Once truth is clear, Dragons proceed.

Long periods of thinking and second-guessing dissipate energy.

Realigning with Wisdom-Key #4: Taking Action

Commitment triggers action. With Wisdom-Keys 1-3, you have made a commitment to live your life with the belief that there is a Grand Plan, that everything that happens to you is part of this Plan and that you and all of creation play a unique and important role in the unfolding of this Grand Plan. Now you need to take action.

Action is the bridge to fully activate your commitment in the world. Because you are embodied, anything you desire must go from Spirit (idea) into form. This is how *you* came into form. From the mind of God, your essence became embodied. This was the Divine taking action to manifest *you*. When you manifest into form, the forgetting process begins. Because it takes so much of your time and energy to maintain life on the material level, you find it difficult to remember that you are Spirit as well as matter. In order to manifest in this realm, that is to put something into action and form, you need to remember that the creation process is bringing Spirit and form together through action.

Sometimes you avoid this step because you are afraid that, if you act, you will make others uncomfortable or angry, or you will appear silly or stupid. You think of yourselves as weak, unheroic and unable to initiate change. You are afraid to make mistakes.

These are all excuses that you make to not take action. But, if you don't act on your commitment, then how do you fulfill your part of the Plan? If you don't act, how do you know who you are because your actions help define who you are? How can you know who you are or what your role in the Divine Plan is unless you make some mistakes, try on some roles and see how they fit?

How did you come to believe that making a mistake means you are a failure? If you don't make mistakes, it means that you are not acting. Rejoice in your mistakes! You often learn much more from mistakes than from successes. Become a *full* participant in your life and in the Divine Plan. Take action now!

Now that you have decided to take action, you need a goal. You know what your *ultimate* goal is, the journey home to God. But, between achieving the ultimate goal and where you are now, there will be many other decisions to be made and goals to be set.

Once you take action and follow a goal, you need to remember to be flexible and to not resist the changes and unexpected twists and turns that life brings you. You have identified a goal, set out on a path or two toward that goal, and began to take action en route. Then, "bam", life happens, and the path that you had chosen is blocked or is impassable due to circumstances beyond mending. This is where flexibility comes to your rescue. You know that there are many ways to achieve a goal and that, because your one chosen path is blocked, it is not necessary for you to abandon the goal. You do not need to say, "Oh poor me! Nothing I do ever turns out. I give up." Or, "I don't know any other way to achieve this goal. I guess I am too unlucky or stupid to achieve my goal." Flexibility can come to the rescue. You are not a victim of misfortune. You are a participant in life, and obstacles are here to test your resolve and to teach you lessons.

You can regroup your energy, calm down, and, if you cannot immediately see another path of action, you can watch and wait. The universe will send you another idea, if you are ready to see it. The goal is what is important. There are many different ways to achieve goals, and often the universe knows better ways than you do in the moment and will supply that information when you are ready. The ultimate goal is the most important, followed by lesser goals along the path. But, circumstances and means can change.

Meditation for Wisdom-Key #4

Take yourself to a quiet place. Sit and make ready. Breathe deeply several times, allowing distractions to melt away. Imagine your Dragon-guide hovering just above you. You can feel the Dragon's gentle and loving gaze, and you begin to relax even more. The Dragon begins to breathe on you. You feel the warm embrace. As your Dragon lands before you, take note of its appearance. You might want to reach out and hug or embrace your Dragon.

Today, the Dragon has plans to teach you an important concept. Just follow the instructions.

The Dragon beckons you to rise from your chair and climb aboard. When you are seated, hold on tightly. You take off out of your room, into the sky, and fly to an unknown landscape. You trust so much that you can close your eyes as the Dragon carries you further. When you begin to slow and glide downward, you look at the meadow where you land.

The meadow appears to be a high one, surrounded by tall pines and ringed with mountains. Wildflowers sway in the breeze. You dismount with the Dragon's help.

Your Dragon says: "There is a task to be accomplished today. Look carefully at the mountains around you. Can you see the castle on the ridge before you? It is not as far as it may seem. Your goal is to reach this castle before midnight. As you can see, a paved road begins in the center of the meadow. You will go first, and I will follow. Lead on."

You run forward and take the paved path that moves through the field toward the rising hills. Your Dragon steps behind you, allowing you to lead.

At one point, as you move near the trees, you see several rocks have piled up on the path. What to do? You begin to lift the rocks and throw them to the side. The Dragon just watches you. When the path is cleared sufficiently, you check the distance to the castle and move forward. The Dragon follows. Now the trees begin to close in around you. No longer are you able to see as clearly. You know the castle lies immediately ahead of you, but the trees obscure the view. Sometimes you can't see the castle at all. What do you do?

You continue to move ahead at a slower pace because the forest is so thick. Suddenly, you come upon several huge trees that have fallen across the paved path.

What to do?

You tug and try to lift but to no avail. They are heavy. Your hands are blistered. You are hot, tired, hungry. You can't even see the castle anymore. What's this all about? Your Dragon just watches. "Come help me," you cry. And the Dragon just smiles.

You tug persistently, but nothing moves. "What should I do? Maybe if I just wait something will happen." You sit on the ground to study the trees and wait and wait. Nothing shifts.

"I've been placed on this path with a mission to reach the castle by midnight, and it's getting late." You wait and wait. The Dragon looks as though it's sleeping, eyes closed, half snoring. "Why is the Dragon no help? God and the Dragon have abandoned me." You wait some more.

Finally, so tired, you fall asleep. You awake with a start, and you look around desperately to see possible routes you didn't see before. "Let's try one of these. There's a path to the right. It's not the main path. Would I be cheating? Would I be unfaithful to my initial instructions? Should I hold on here no matter what?" And so, you sit and wait. Meanwhile, the Dragon appears to be enjoying his nap.

You rise up again and again to attempt to lift the trees, but they simply won't budge. What to do?

The Dragon seems to be no help at all, and you want to scream. You are frustrated and angry. "Oh, so what. I'm ready to try another way out of this mess. After all, I need to get to the castle."

You rise up, step off the paved path and move to the path you first saw when you woke.

You almost forget about your Dragon as you hurry forward. But, as you turn, you see your Dragon happily trotting behind you.

Within moments, you see the trees open out into a huge area surrounding the castle. You made it!

The Dragon grabs your hands and dances around with you. "You made it. You made it."

"Now, what did you learn?"

You sit down right there with your Dragon.

Your Dragon asks you, "What did you learn? What did this experience teach you about achieving a goal and the means of achieving that goal?"

When you are ready, the Dragon will return you to your home and to your chair. You are free to note down all that you have learned. Your Dragon flies off while the teachings remain to deepen within you.

Tools for Integration of Wisdom-Key #4

1. *Affirmations/Positive Self-Messages*—Repeat two times per day for two weeks:

   a. I turn my commitments into action in my life.

   b. I can set realistic goals and act on them.

   c. I have the courage to find new and creative ways to solve problems.

   d. Making mistakes is how I learn about myself and the world.

   e. I accept the situations that life brings to me and make adjustments as needed.

2. *Journaling*—Take some quiet time and write from your own life experiences:

   a. What excuses do I make for not being an active participant in my life? What do I do to keep a low-profile so no one notices me?

   b. Do I ignore and belittle my personal gifts as an excuse to not act? How can I change that?

   c.   Do I have immediate and long-range goals in my life? What are they? Have I manifested some of my past goals? Which ones?

   d.   How did these goals become realized? Were there obstacles to overcome? How did I overcome them?

   e.   In what areas do I feel forward movement? Where do I feel stuck?

   f.   Journal about times when you have felt stuck and what new approaches could have been used to move forward.

3. *Other Activities*—These are different ways to integrate this Wisdom-Key:

   a.   Think about situations in your life where action has been needed and you failed to act. What were the consequences?

   b.   Taking action can also mean establishing boundaries. Are there, or have there been, times when you allowed your boundaries to be violated because you did not act to protect yourself? What could you do differently now?

   c.   Find three or four alternative ways of handling a current issue in your life.

   d.   Observe current political or religious issues that highlight either rigidity or flexibility.

   e.   Change one aspect of your daily routine and observe what happens.

   f.   Choose a physical activity (e.g. yoga, dancing, Tai Chi) that requires adaptability and teaches new ways to move.

g. Walk a labyrinth and experience what it teaches about changing course and achieving goals.

Wisdom Key #5: Abundance

There is true abundance for all. When you are in balance and aligned, abundance is yours.

The Illusion We Live With

You know there are limited resources in the world. Not everyone can have what they want. In order for you to get everything that you need and want, you must fight for it. Competition is the name of the game, and you must be quick and smart and greedy to survive well.

You also know that material and spiritual abundance are different. Material abundance is about money, assets and worldly power. People who are after material abundance are not people who care about spiritual matters because it makes them soft and takes their eye off the prize.

Spiritual abundance is about wanting a connection with God, to the unseen world, and wanting to live a life of service, truth, compassion and love. These people don't want power or material wealth because it pollutes their spiritual quest.

How This Illusion Impacts Society and the World

When you, as an individual or a nation, believe that there is a limited amount of resources in the world and act accordingly, then the message you are giving to the universe is that there is not enough for everyone and for every nation. This brings about a self-fulfilling prophecy where the universe matches your beliefs. This belief can often lead to hoarding which further reinforces the message that there is not enough, because you have more than you could every use and others go without.

In addition, you have again allowed yourselves to see matter and Spirit as separate and disconnected. You live your lives according to the fundamental misconception that you can either have material wealth and worldly power *or* spiritual purity. Nonsense!

This destructive way of defining abundance as either material *or* spiritual has allowed governments and corporations to rape the earth and oppress its people in the name of greed and the bottom line. Because, when you believe that material and spiritual abundance are different and not connected, humans often completely disregard the results of their actions and do anything in the name of making money and wielding power. It is *never okay* to hurt others or the earth to make a profit or gain power.

However, when you look at material abundance as corrupt and unholy, then you deny your material nature. If you believe that being poor and lacking power makes you spiritual, then aren't you mirroring to the world that *spirit* is poor and lacks power? On this earth, Spirit must move through matter. If the spiritual person stays on the sidelines and refuses to get involved in the marketplace, then Spirit becomes irrelevant and marginalized.

Both these positions lead to excesses. Believing in only material abundance causes selfish actions that disregard consequences to others (e.g., polluting rivers for material gain, exploiting workers for company profits). The excesses of spiritual purity disregard the needs and the joys of the physical world. The body and the physical are considered to be temptations, rather than another expression of the Divine. In the zeal to communicate with Spirit, it is easy to overlook the needs of the body and ignore the Divine in the body that you live in. When you allow Spirit to work through matter, you can achieve a *new bottom line* where both worlds are honored.

The Dragons' Fire Message

My friends, the great secret is that all reality is of the Divine. There is nothing separate and apart. The great Homecoming cannot happen until you realize this and respect *all* in whatever form it appears. Why such difficulties with money and other forms of wealth? It is because man introduced greed and possessiveness into the world. It was then that teachings developed to say that the material world and its riches were the *all*, and in opposition to this, religious structures taught the evils of wealth. This has resulted in inequities across the world as well as guilt and resentment. Isn't it time you saw the truth? As children of the One, all that the Divine manifests is yours and belongs to all. We have guarded the truth for eons, guarded the *true* treasure. We discern it wherever it hides. Your role is to align with the truth of your being and to manifest it in your lives. When this happens, all is in Divine order and abundance can flow.

Realigning with Wisdom-Key #5: Abundance

As a co-creator of the Divine Plan, you are an heir to all abundance. But most of humanity measures abundance using only one scale of measurement. You measure abundance using an either/or method. But, humanity, and all of creation, is both/and. You are both matter and Spirit. There is no separation. They are different parts of the whole. Matter *is* Spirit incarnated. When you honor both Spirit and matter, you connect yourselves to all of creation, and abundance from all of creation flows into your lives. Look at the abundance all around you. Abundance can be seen in your relationships, in the diversity of the natural world and in the great achievements of human culture-great music, literature, art and science. You exist in the middle of this great abundance, yet you only allow yourselves to see and value a small part of it. You are out of balance when you do this.

To achieve balance or alignment, it is necessary to bring the truth of your limitless essence into your thoughts, emotions and body. When your thoughts and beliefs mirror "lack", this influences your emotions and your physical body and what you manifest in the physical world. When the mind gives you messages "that there is not enough for all", your emotions react with fear, your body constricts and your attention narrows so that you only see what is missing in your life and in the world. Your energy then takes on the message that there is not enough in the world for everyone. This creates the manifestation of your belief that there is not enough. When you realign to the Truth, that you are of God and that God is limitless and that there is enough for everyone, you change your thoughts, your fearful emotions lift, your body relaxes, and you see the abundance that is around you. Then, you manifest your new vision.

As the Christian scriptures say, "Where your treasure is, there also will your heart be." Dragons know this to be true and are asking you more clearly to identify the treasures in your lives so that you don't waste your time and energy chasing and hording false treasure. Dragons have been traditionally associated with guarding wealth, and it was presumed that this meant that Dragons were greedy and interested in only material wealth. This is a complete misunderstanding of Dragons' motives and characters.

Dragons know that it is important to cultivate both spiritual and material wealth in your lives. If you don't, you lose access to one half of the abundance of the universe. If you allow either the material definition of abundance and success *or* the spiritual definition of abundance and success to be the *only* definitions, then you lose balance in your lives. Discernment allows you to understand that spiritual and material abundance are inseparable and equally important in living a successful life. Consider the following:

- How important is material wealth when you have an incurable illness? Money does pay for health care, but it cannot help you when there is no cure.

- How important is money when you wish to increase your wisdom and compassion? Money can buy you books, tapes, CD's and can take you to lectures given by wise people, but money does not open your hearts to become compassionate and wise.

- Some people believe that being wealthy makes it more difficult or even impossible to have spiritual abundance. Does being poor help you to attain a higher level of spiritual abundance? If you are worried about money and do not know how you will buy food for this week, how does that bring you closer to the Source? When you are worried about how to pay the rent, how to fix the car, how to sustain your physical being, then you are preoccupied with the lack of material abundance and are not able to give much if any attention to your spiritual lives. Since you are both physical and spiritual, isn't it essential that you recognize all parts of yourselves and therefore recognize that you need both spiritual and material abundance to feed your spirits *and* bodies?

Discernment allows you to see and acknowledge all the abundance that exists in your lives and to know that both your financial and spiritual assets need to be recognized and cared for. You know that material wealth is important to pay the bills and support your physical lives, and you know that your spiritual wealth supports your non-physical lives. Discernment helps you to know where you are out of balance and what parts of your lives need to be emphasized or de-emphasized. Discernment allows you to fully appreciate all and not ignore or discount the financial or spiritual aspects of your lives. Your Homeward journey is enhanced by both realms. If you separate spiritual and financial abundance, you limit yourselves. Together, they open unlimited possibilities.

Meditation for Wisdom-Key #5

Sit in a quiet place, close your eyes and call your special Dragon to you. You may feel a wind swirling around you as the huge wings of your friend stir up the air. Your Dragon can lower its wings so that you may climb up for a journey into the world of abundance. When you are ready to proceed, climb up and hold on tightly. Feel yourself rise up and glide into the sky, trusting that you will be protected.

You move through clouds that are thick and milky in color. Then, before you know it, you emerge from the clouds to see rocky cliffs in the distance. There is a valley floor below and the cliffs are high above...so high that you think you can see eagles nesting above you.

You see a great waterfall in the distance. It spills over the crest of the cliff, full and tumultuous, sending mist everywhere. The Dragon glides close to the water, so close you can feel the spray on your face. Then, he swiftly moves behind the waters and enters a cave opening on the face of the cliff.

At first, the cave seems dark, cold and empty. But, as your eyes adjust and you move deeper within, you see some light and feel some warmth, and the noise of the waters grows quieter.

The Dragon places you on the ground and stands beside you. The cave is very large, looming high over the Dragon's head. There are places where water drips and forms small pools. Your Dragon tells you, "This cave was once, long ago, formed by the waters you see here. We come here to reflect on abundance. Follow me."

At that, your Dragon pushes you with its nose, over to an area that is recessed against the far walls of the cave. As you get closer, you see that it resembles a separate room. You move inside together.

The Dragon says to you, "Look around at what is here."

You see what looks like a great treasure room, filled from top to bottom with chests whose contents spill out...chests of gold, of gemstones, of silver. You see pieces of art and sculpture, as well as piles of sheet music. You see examples of nature's abundance: species of flowers, plants, animals-alive or in picture form. You see images of oceans, mountains and deserts. You see pictures that show compassion, warmth, generosity. You see images of the diversity of mankind and pictures that express joy and celebration.

The Dragon says, "This is a treasure-trove, a secret place where one can see the treasures that the Divine has given to His children. This represents abundance for those who know the secret. I will take you now to see the secret."

With that, the Dragon swoops you up onto its back, and the Dragon flies out of the cave entrance, away from the falls and up to the top of the cliff.

There, you can see and hear the loud pounding of the rushing river that moves swiftly. The river is so full that the water is churned up with froth and rushes onward. Your Dragon flies higher and higher, further and further, until you reach a point where you can look down and see two rivers that feed into the rushing waters. When you travel more miles, you are only aware of these two bodies of water, seemingly far apart from one another on the landscape.

The Dragon flies higher and further until you see great mountains in the distance, snow-covered and majestic. As you get closer to these mountains, you are able to see one river again flowing from the mountains, cold and icy.

Your Dragon says, "Look toward the source. The river begins here in the heights. Then, as you have seen, it branches into two great rivers. And, eventually, comes together again. There are those who have lived along one of these rivers for ages and who no longer know that they are the same river. To know the secret, you must travel and have vision to be able to see the Truth."

"This is the same teaching about matter and spirit." Your Dragon says, "In the same way, mankind has forgotten that matter and Spirit are from the One Source. They may appear to be different, but one who knows the secret, and gets the vision, knows that they must come together again for abundance to fill the world."

At that, the Dragon flies smoothly and very quickly back to the point where the two rivers merge. He follows the one, powerful river to the point where it roars over the cliff-face and pours in the waterfall down to the valley floor.

He dives down with you atop his back until you land in a spot where the water has collected in a small pool. He says, "Remember that the abundance cave was formed by these balanced waters. You may bathe in these waters now."

The Dragon helps you to dismount, and you are able to carefully move into the waters which are surprisingly warm. This is no ordinary place because these waters hold the secrets of the oneness of matter and Spirit and the true secrets of abundance.

Let yourself nestle down here in the waters so that they embrace you. Affirm that you are allowing your desire for balance and alignment to be present and fill you, while any false illusions are washed away. Ask to receive your true birthright as a child of the One. Ask that these waters "carve you out"--as they did the cave-- as a vessel to hold the abundance of the universe. Ask that these waters of Divine energy-*your energy*-flow now with power and force to create your life as you want it to be. Feel the force flowing through you without resistance or blocks, like the waters flowing over the cliff-face. Remember, when there is alignment, when your energy field matches the Truth of you, there is nothing to prevent the fullness that you are heir to from filling your life.

When you are ready to emerge from the waters, climb up on the rocks at the edges of this pool where your Dragon waits. The sun's rays dry you and warm you.

Your Dragon lets you know that you may return here at any time to assist your energy to reflect the truth of who you are.

You climb aboard the Dragon's back, and the Dragon takes you home.

Tools for integration of Wisdom-Key #5

1. *Affirmations/Positive Self-Messages*—Repeat two times per day for two weeks:
    a. As I move into fullness and balance, abundance flows automatically in my life.
    b. I open myself to the flow of abundant living, both in receiving and in giving.
    c. My wealth and resources allow my spiritual service to increase and prosper.
    d. I hold sacred all that comes from the Source, material as well as spiritual.
    e. There are no limits to the abundance that is mine.
    f. Through my intention and actions I draw balance and discernment into my life.

2. *Journaling*—Take some quiet time and write from your own life experiences:

    a. When you hear the word "abundance" what do you think? What do physical abundance, emotional abundance, mental abundance and spiritual abundance mean to you?

    b. Where do you see abundance in your life now? Its absence?

    c. If you were to list your life's priorities, what would they be? Which would you categorize as material, spiritual? Do these priorities support your ultimate goal?

    d. If you feel out of balance, how would you begin to regain a balance point where the material and spiritual feed one another?

    e. How do you honor the sacredness of the material world (your body, animals, plants, the earth)?

    f. Do you believe that abundance is limited? If so, how does this effect your life?

3. *Other Activities*—These are different ways to integrate this Wisdom-Key:

    a. You might want to check in your bookstore or library about books that are related to abundance consciousness (prosperity, etc.)

    b. Look under www.google.com. There are millions of references to matter and Spirit, as well as millions of references to abundance. Be aware of the many quick money schemes in the abundance category.

    c. As you look at TV, listen to the radio, read magazines and newspapers, look for what our culture values and for what values leads us to imbalance and unhappiness.

Wisdom-Key #6: Non-attachment and Lightness

You are supported by the universe. When you are unattached to outcome and let go, all things come to you.

The Illusion We Live With

By holding tightly to people or situations, I can mold those people or situations to my will/expectations. I know what is best, and I will make it happen.

Also, by holding tightly to a person or an outcome, I am showing how important that person or outcome/goal is to me. Attachment shows what is important to me and what I can count on.

I know that the way to keep happiness in my life is to hold tightly to all my achievements and possessions. Also, when I stay attached to mistakes and shame I will remember not to do those things again and not to take risks in life. In fact, my very identity is a valuable attachment. This identity that was given to me by family, friends and the culture tells me who I am. If I don't believe what they tell me, I risk not knowing myself.

How This Illusion Impacts Society and the World

When you hold on tightly to anything, you strangle what you value because you don't allow growth and change. When you attach tightly to love, you become possessive and jealous and drive away love. When you attach to looking for justice, you can become filled with feelings of revenge that destroy your life. When you attach to mistakes and shame, you feel hopeless, stupid and worthless. You become afraid to act because you may make another mistake. When you attach to an identity, given you by others, you cheat yourselves. You are afraid to change, to grow and to find out who you really are.

What happens when societies act in a similar way? Countries and societies get stuck just like individuals. Attachments cloud vision. You no longer can see situations as they are. Look at the attachment called racism. You judge people by the color of the skin, not by who they really are. Look at the attachment called sexism. Females are seen as property and believed to be inferior to males in all areas of life. A society loses half of its resources by attaching to this belief.

When societies are not blinded by their attachments, it would be possible to let in compassion and new approaches to solving old problems. Without attachment, it is possible to think "out of the box".

What would a society look like if it acted in accord with the principle of lightness or non-attachment? Such a society would support new ideas; it would honor the beliefs and customs of others; it would negotiate differences rather than wage war; it would be able to view clearly its own mistakes and change course as needed; and it would not allow old hatreds to determine decisions or actions.

Is this too idealistic? Is this impossible? No. A new world can be created if you are willing to let go of all the things which blind you and narrow your view and make it impossible to be here now.

The Dragons' Fire Message

Beloved Ones: We have watched mankind for so long! And, we have watched your ambitions to fly beyond what has been seen and known before, to push the limits of the known world. We know a great deal about flying above and beyond. We want to share with you some principles of common sense that you need to see more clearly. How can you fly anywhere when you are tightly tethered to the ground, bound to heavy anchors that pull you back every time you seek to rise? You understand this when we talk of planes or balloons, but you don't always see when this applies to factors in your life that hold you captive. There are things you think you cannot live without. There are things that fill your life that need your constant care and attention. There are people and things that hold fast to you, even beyond any necessity. There are concerns that absorb your attention, riches you need to guard, reputations you need to uphold, and roles you need to feed. These are no less tethers than the blocks that tie aircraft to the ground. To risk having the all is to risk letting go. Lighten up!

Realigning with Wisdom-Key #6: Non-attachment and Lightness

Attachments are easy to make and are a necessary part of being in a body. This is a basic condition of the material world. In fact, healthy development in an infant involves the ability to form a strong attachment to a parental figure. This foundation makes it possible to develop a healthy ego and an ability later in life to become independent.

But being *overly* attached presents problems. "To attach" comes from the medieval English word that means "to nail." What in your life are you "nailed" to, or what have other people "nailed" to you?

Attachments that you are "nailed" to make you rigid. Your world view becomes so narrow that it is not possible to look at another version of reality. Attachments anchor you to your personality and block the flow of Spirit's wisdom. Any attachment impedes the flow of energy, but the stronger the attachment, the more constricted the energy flow becomes. Addictions are an extreme form of unhealthy attachments.

Unhealthy attachments make you rigid and "nail" you to certain points of view, beliefs and behaviors. An unhealthy attachment is marked by extreme dependence, the need to control, possessiveness, ownership, and an inability to function if deprived of the attachment.

The difference between a healthy and non-healthy attachment is the difference between being "nailed" to something or using velcro. The attachment that is "nailed" to you cannot be removed without lots of pain and resistance. A connection that is more velcroed is a connection or attachment that is like a preference. If it needs to be removed or adjusted, you can do it fairly easily and move on. The latter is a healthy attachment or connection that you are not cemented to.

The attachments of individuals flow out and affect the thinking and actions of an entire society. Masses of people in a culture can be pulled into holding similar thoughts, opinions, and prejudices. These attachments can be either positive or negative. The Bill of Rights in the U.S. Constitution can be viewed as a positive attachment to the basic rights of all people. The pressure to feel a certain way, think a certain way, be and act in a certain way in a society or culture can be overwhelming. But, this pressure can be overcome. The Dragons bring support for change, starting with the individual and moving out to whole peoples. **You can be free**.

How do you recognize your attachments? Begin by looking at what you are passionate about, what you desire, where you feel stuck, what you most care about and what upsets you. These are the places where your attachments are most probably anchored.

Once you recognize your attachments, how do you go

about loosening them? The first step is recognition. Once you are aware, hold the intention to loosen the attachment. (For further suggestions, please see "Other Activities" at the end of this chapter.) Moving toward detachment is not moving toward a sterile uncaring place. Detachment means "objectivity with love". You can be attached to many different categories of things, objects, people, emotions, beliefs, and thoughts. When you begin this detachment process, choose an attachment to work with that does not carry a great deal of emotional weight.

Perhaps your most rigid and strongly held attachment is to who you think you are. When others and society tell you who you should be, you judge and compare yourself to standards that tell you that you are always lacking and that being who you truly are is not enough. Because you believe these standards to be true, you become filled with anger, fear, and resentment, and you try harder and harder to reach these standards and move further and further away from your *true self*. So much energy is used in keeping this false identity in place that you are unable to live in the present.

When you are freed up from your unhealthy attachments, it brings lightness, flexibility and the ability to stay in the present and be more clear.

Meditation for Wisdom-Key #6

Sit or lie down in a comfortable position and let your body relax. Take a few deep breaths and settle. Call to your Dragon. Your Dragon is ready to tell you the long- held Dragon secret of lightness and flying. Climb onto your Dragon's back and off you go into the air. Hold on tightly as your Dragon is going to do some tricks. Tell your Dragon what you would like, a loop-de-loop, a very fast dive, a very fast ascent, a spiral, whatever you and your Dragon want to do together.

After the exciting flying, you and your Dragon fly to a

high plateau that has a wonderful view of the two rivers of matter and Spirit that are rushing down below. Your Dragon begins to tell you how Dragons fly and how you too can learn to fly.

Your Dragon says: "When you are not overly attached, you are in balance and all things are possible. When you honor both the material and the spiritual, you are whole, and the universe opens to you. When you honor both matter and Spirit, you are not overly attached to either and, therefore, can be light. The Dragons learned this truth long ago. Though some of our species are very large and heavy, we can fly because we are centered and balanced. We have learned that, if you become attached to only matter or only Spirit--one *or* the other-- it causes heaviness and confusion and anchors you to illusion. When you are in balance, you are light, and clear and able to fly."

Your Dragon continues: "Are you attached to fear, anger, resentment, feelings of unworthiness, or any feeling or belief that causes a heaviness or feeling of being trapped? Are you ready to release these attachments or these ways of reacting?"

If you are ready to release, think about how you react to life's challenges. Do you meet your challenges with anger, resentment, feelings of being unworthy? How do you act and feel when under the influence of these beliefs/attachments? Give yourself some time to really feel this. Then, with awareness, tell yourself that you no longer need to react in this way. Forgive yourself and these beliefs for the dis-ease they have caused.

Place the beliefs/attachments in front of your Dragon and ask your Dragon to breathe its violet flames over them. When you look again, there is a pile of ashes. Take the ashes of the transformed beliefs and throw them from the plateau into the place where the rivers of Spirit and matter join and cascade over the cliff.

How do you feel?

Take some time to experience what has happened. Perhaps you don't feel anything right now. It may take days or weeks for you to experience this release. The attachment you chose will begin to loosen. You will be aware more quickly when this attachment begins to operate in you. As you become aware of this attachment in action, you will be able to choose another way to act. You will no longer react without thinking when you face a challenge in your life. You will be able to use all your talents to face a challenge instead of reacting in the usual way. You will become more flexible and able to see yourself differently.

Remember that this transformational violet fire is available to you whenever you are ready to release more of your attachments. You can either ask your Dragon to breathe the violet flame, or you can do it yourself. Visualize a violet fire and then put your attachments into the fire, and they will burn and turn to ash.

You have begun the process of releasing those ties that bind you to heaviness. Prepare to fly!

Tools for Integration of Wisdom-Key #6

1. *Affirmations/Positive Self-Messages*—Repeat two times per day for two weeks:
   a. I release with ease, and for my highest good, anything that has become a rigid attachment for me.
   b. Any addictions in my life become clear so that I can begin to detach.
   c. I experience lightness and clarity as I forgive and release my unhealthy attachments.
   d. As I release rigid attachments, the process

becomes easier.

2.   *Journaling*—Take some quiet time and write from your own life experiences:

    a. Are there areas of your life where you feel stuck, for example, in relationships with others, in certain belief systems? Which specific things, people, roles, behaviors, beliefs are most intense and would be very difficult to loosen or release? Which would be moderately difficult? How would you "un-stick" yourself? What forces or people would try and keep you stuck?

    b. Do you habitually react to challenges in the same manner which hinders rather than helps you cope? For example, when faced with a challenge, is your first response anger, fear, or paralysis? How would you change this?

    c. Imagine yourself and your life as ideal. Describe how you and your life would be. What prevents you from living your ideal? Do you say to yourself, "I'm too stupid," "I don't deserve this," "I'm not good enough."?

    d. How does your attachment to your personality/ego hinder your identification with the Spirit that you are?

    e. Write down at least three positive and at least three not so positive characteristics of your personality, for example, impatient, loving, gentle, aggressive, giving, manipulative. When were these characteristics used to describe you? Who described you by using these words? Your parents, your friend, your teacher? Do these characteristics really describe you? What characteristics do? Who do you think you are in the world? How would friends, peers describe you?

f. What challenges would come up for you if you tried to release an old pattern or prized possession or mark of your identity in the world?

g. If others' perceptions of you were withdrawn, what would be left of the true you?

3. *Other Activities*—These are different ways to integrate this Wisdom-Key:

   a. Cultivate awareness. Choose an attachment that you wish to release. Keep it simple at first.

   b. Write an affirmation about the release of the chosen attachment. Read this two times per day for six weeks.

   c. Do a short, daily visualization of the release process and of your life without this attachment. Do this for six weeks.

   d. When you become aware of how the old attachment works in your everyday life, choose a new way of thinking or acting.

   e. You might want to read about addictions that may take many diverse forms. Are any of these true for you?

   f. Readings about attachment and detachment might be helpful. Look at Buddhist texts.

Wisdom Key #7: Compassion

We are all in this together. Be kind to yourself and others.

The Illusion We Live With

I am a separate being, with my own goals. To achieve my goals, I must concentrate on myself. Compassion is foolish because it draws my attention to others and their misfortunes. Others' misfortunes are not my concern, and I can't help anyway. Besides, showing compassion to myself or others just shows weakness. People need to be judged for their failures, and wrong actions, not excused for them.

How This Illusion Impacts Society and the World

A lack of compassion, kindness or thoughtfulness makes the individual as well as the society and the world mean, nasty, and unforgiving. You step over the homeless, thinking that they deserve the life they are living and label them as lazy. You allow millions to starve when grain rots in fields. You allow genocide to occur in the world. You believe that the suffering of others has no relationship to you.

A lack of compassion and a belief that you are separate from one another cause harsh judgments. When you judge and condemn according to these standards, there is no room to make mistakes or to be human. When you judge and condemn, you see only shortcomings and flaws. This creates a distorted view of yourself and others and leads to self-hatred and disrespect that paves the way to conflict and war. To believe in the oneness of all creation allows compassion to blossom and radically shifts attitudes and behaviors.

The Dragons' Fire Message

Beloved Friends and Students, we look very different

from you, and yet we know that we are not separate or distinct. We know that we are all varied images of the One, inhabiting this planet. The experience of one is the experience of all. Your lives echo one anothers'. The way you respond is so much the same because you are all experiencing life. Because this is true, the pain of one is the pain of all, just as the joy of one is the joy of all. Life experiences itself through each one of you. This is the basis of that most beautiful gift of compassion. You are able to feel and support one another as you all experience life. This is the gift that enables you all to feel the pain and joys of others. To withhold compassion from another is to withhold it from yourself when you most need it. Compassion flows only when you know the truth of the great Divine Plan and experience it operating *inside* you. It is the overflowing of truth to one another!

Realigning with Wisdom Key #7: Compassion

You often forget to be compassionate to yourselves, and that is where compassion begins. Since you are part of creation, you deserve compassion. For generations, religious traditions have taught more about compassion toward others and labeled attention to yourselves as selfish. Compassion begins at home. If you are harsh and judgmental with yourselves, you tend to be the same with others. If you are forgiving and respectful of yourselves, you are more likely to give this to others as well. Self-compassion creates a gentle understanding of the difficulties of living a human life.

Self-compassion easily leads to compassion for others. Compassion means to "feel together" or to "suffer together". Is this not what you humans do? You all face illness and death, of yourselves and of loved ones. You all face the ravages of natural and man-made disasters such as volcanoes, floods, starvation and war. Your faces show the same expressions for love, hate and confusion. You share the same DNA. Yet, you insist on believing and acting as if you are separate, not only from each other, but also from animals, plants and the earth. Even the most simple form of one-celled life on earth and you share 50% of the same DNA.

You often feel the oneness of human experience when facing a disaster, but then quickly revert to believing that you have nothing in common with one another. You see yourselves as separate material beings who are in competition for everything. But, in fact, you share the same needs and the same emotions. Your bodies share the same chemical composition. You are affected by the physics of earth in the same way. Everyone is affected by gravity, the same rain, sun and air. The same air eventually finds its way to all parts of the planet.

Not only are you so very similar on the physical/material plane, but you are all of God. In the face of so many similarities, how can you still believe that you are each separate from one another? How have you allowed the illusion of separateness to become so strong and compelling? Look at the world that you have constructed with these beliefs of separateness, a world that allows millions to starve to death; a world that allows the stronger to wage war on the weaker; a world that rewards selfishness and greed no matter who or what is hurt in the process; a world that devalues the principles of love, gentleness, acceptance, forgiveness, generosity and compassion itself.

The practice of compassion allows you to experience the oneness of all life on Earth. You all want to be physically safe, happy, well fed, and free to develop your individual talents. You all want companionship and to love and be loved. Isn't it easier to accomplish these goals when you are all working together instead of tearing each other apart? The answer seems so simple, yet it seems as far away as it has ever been. Now, with world-wide communication and travel made so much easier, isn't it time for your similarities to become greater than your differences?

When you see yourselves as separate from other humans, as well as separate from other forms of life, you allow yourselves to be manipulated into a competitive "when I win, you lose" mentality. You isolate yourselves and sink into loneliness and despair. You have allowed yourselves to fall victim to the "divide and conquer" tactics of modern day politics. It is time to see the totality of life on earth as just that--a totality--that is interdependent and interrelated and not separate and apart. Your lives depend on it!

The compassion that is needed at this time is unconditional and unlimited. It flows naturally from the Truth of the oneness of all creation. This flow of compassion to others goes to all: the murderer, the thief, the abuser, the addict, the powerful and the weak.

Compassion should be given to all because compassion recognizes the God in all of us. It is not based on behavior or status in the world. No matter what the behavior, we all need to be treated with dignity and respect. It is only common sense that murderers, thieves and others that hurt their fellow humans need to be separated out. But, prisons should not consider prisoners as less than human. You all have God inside, and all, prisoners as well, need to have that fact honored and respected. Prisons should not torture or maltreat.

Compassion should flow to all of creation, not just to humans. Spirit gives compassion to all with a free and open heart. But, the world often gives compassion according to its judgments and standards. When you act in a worldly manner, you plunder and ravage Mother Earth, taking her resources and hoarding them for profit. When you act with compassion, you share what is there and take into account the needs of future generations.

Meditation for Wisdom Key #7

Go to your special quiet place. Close your eyes and breathe deeply. Your Dragon guide comes to you as you relax and move inward.

Climb aboard your Dragon's back. Your Dragon is about to take you into the presence of the sacred structure of creation. The Dragon flies upward and all you experience is swift movement, as well as changes in the light. As you travel beyond the view of everyday vision, you notice the sky becoming darker. You begin to see points of pearlescent light around you, and you know you are immersed in an eternal blanket of stars.

Your Dragon flies even higher. Then, the Dragon says:

"Behold your planet from space. From here, you can more easily observe the truth. You all live together on this small blue-green planet. You all must share the resources of this planet because that is all you have. Notice that you cannot see the boundaries that separate countries. You see only the different colors of land and water, the cloud cover of your atmosphere, the shifting patterns of day and night as your Earth rotates. From this point of view, it is easier to see that all the oceans are connected, that eventually all breathe the same air! Your planet is a small jewel hung in the vast expanse of the universe.

Humans rarely see this entire picture because their view is limited. They see only their own small part of the web of life. Because of their limited vision, human societies and cultures make up their own versions of what is true and of who matters most and of who and what is to be outcast and ignored.

When your vision is unlimited, you can see that,

if you touch one part of the great web of life, the entire web moves. If one part of the web is damaged, the entire web suffers."

Now, hovering in space, your Dragon asks you to fill yourself with compassion and love for this small planet and for all life on it. The Dragon asks you to send this love and compassion through your heart in the form of a rose/pink cloud that will embrace the entire planet and be absorbed *into* the planet. Remember to include yourself in this. Watch as the cloud embraces the planet and begins to sink in to bring comfort and compassion to all suffering on Planet Earth.

Sit for a few minutes and continue to send this loving compassion to all and to yourself as well.

Then, the Dragon unfurls its wings, and you travel homeward. You hang on tightly, often closing your eyes in flight. When you open your eyes, you see your everyday world. The Dragon swoops downward and brings you home.

Rest now, reflecting on all that these teachings could mean in your life and in your world.

Tools for Integration of Wisdom Key #7

1. *Affirmations/Positive Self-Messages*—Repeat two times per day for two weeks:
   a. I experience compassion for all beings, even when I don't agree or understand their beliefs or behaviors.
   b. I see more clearly the interrelatedness of all and act with that in mind.
   c. I support political action and economic decisions that are based on compassion and that treat all people with respect.
   d. Because I am one with all creation, I act compassionately toward all, including myself.

2. *Journaling*—Take some quiet time and write from your own life experiences:
   a. What changes would you need to make in your thinking to see the interconnectedness of life?
   b. What compassionate acts have you performed in the last few months? What was your motivation?
   c. Think of a time when someone needed your compassion and you did not give it. Explain. Was there anything you could have believed differently that would have enabled you to be compassionate?
   d. If you truly saw other humans, plants, animals and the Earth as part of your family, how would your behavior change?

3. *Other Activities*—These are different ways to integrate this Wisdom-Key:
   a. Follow the workings of the United Nations or any charitable agency more closely. Look at their work from the point of view of compassion.
   b. Find some ways that true compassion might enhance some local community views or projects. How can you help achieve this?
   c. Read about Metta or Loving-Kindness meditation. Consult books by Sharon Salzburg, the Dali Lama and other Buddhist authors.
   d. Learn about the interrelatedness of life by reading books by authors such as Joanna Macy, and Native American philosophies, biological or DNA studies.
   e. Begin by doing a compassionate act once a week/month. Some examples are: volunteering at a charitable organization, helping a neighbor, friend or family member, donating food, clothing

or money, smiling at others every day, driving with respect toward other motorists.

Wisdom-Key #8: Gratitude and Joy

Feel grateful for all you are and have, and joy will fill you.

The Illusion We Live With

If you see life as it really is, how can you be grateful? How can you live in this world and not see that life is hard work with lots of pain and problems? And, you so rarely get what you want! As soon as one problem is solved, another one takes its place. What is there to be grateful for? What is there to be joyful about? Gratitude and joy are qualities of those who have their heads "in the clouds."

How This Illusion Impacts Society and the World

When you are so busy looking at what you don't have and what problems there are in your life, you fail to see all that you really *do* have, and you fail to see that your problems don't make you a victim. Without gratitude for all that you have, your world becomes dark and negative. You feel lost, abandoned, victimized and desperate. You are unable to appreciate or value all the wonders around you and the wonder that you *are* as an aspect of God. Without gratitude in your life, you lash out at others because you covet the happiness that others seem to have. Because you don't value what you already have, you see the good fortune of others as unattainable and unfair to *you*.

When you are dissatisfied, you wonder, if you had what "Jane or Joe" have, would you be happy? So, you strive to get what they have. And, since you don't feel gratitude or value anything, even this does not satisfy you. And, so it goes!

When you feel locked into this way of viewing your life, you are unable to experience gratitude for *anything*. A lack of gratitude causes constant dissatisfaction. You don't appreciate or value what you have or who you are. You go through "stuff" and relationships like kleenex. Nothing seems to fill the void, and you never have any peace. You strive, achieve and are dissatisfied over and over again.

Dissatisfaction also leads to more covetousness. Covetousness can easily change to anger, jealousy and feelings of victimization, causing more problems for yourself and others.

The inability to feel gratitude for what you do have and coveting what others seem to have that makes them happy, produces the same results in nations as in individuals. The irony of this is that wealthy nations are often the ones that seem to suffer from a lack of gratitude and from more and more desires.

When countries are unable to appreciate and value what they do have, they start wars to get more, or they damage the entire ecosystem of the planet in their attempt to satisfy their cravings. Social unrest and jealousy among classes of people and nations are created because of the inequality in the accumulation of things, such as more land, more power and more consumer goods. These cravings, and all that result, never end because there is no ultimate satisfaction.

Cultivating gratitude in an individual and in a nation's ethos would do much to change the suffering and conflict on this planet!

The Dragons' Fire Message

Dearest Ones, We want to let you know that it is essential that you express gratitude for who you are and for all that you have been given. Yes, of course, there are problems that you must cope with, but you have been given the birthright of Kings. You are the heirs of the Divine! Gratitude is *your* response for such a privilege. It is your acknowledgement of the gifts that have been showered upon you. If you aren't able to see the outpouring of these gifts all around you and within you, you are not truly alive. Without this ability to be thankful, you can never allow joy to overwhelm you. Without gratitude, you box yourselves in to a shadowy existence, unable to see the light that is all around and unable to feel the joy that wants to rise up in you.

Joy *does* exist, but you cannot experience it until you are able to see clearly that you are blessed! Joy is a nectar that can't be bought or paid for. Joy comes from being able to acknowledge the rightness of all creation and of all events and situations. It comes in its own timing as a result of consistent trust, surrender and thanksgiving. It abides with those who seek their true identity and their true heritage as children of the One.

Gratitude, and its resulting joy, are the natural inheritance of those who have remembered and know themselves to be in deep union with the One, the Source of all. Joy comes when all anxiety and striving end because there is no need to work to possess that which you already have!

It is our greatest desire that you all abide in the gratitude and joy that is everlasting, allowing the truth to unfold within you and burn brightly. Gratitude and joy, serenity and love bubble up from you because they could not do otherwise. Open, allow, relax, see the truth and give thanks. Let joy fill you!

Realigning With Wisdom-Key #8: Gratitude and Joy

If you count your blessings, you begin to experience gratitude, and joy fills you. By "gratitude," we do not mean the feeling you have when you are indebted to someone because they did you a service. We mean a gratitude that has a larger focus and scope. We are talking about gratitude that comes from knowing that you are always supported by God and all of creation. Do you ever give thanks for the sun and rain that fall on the earth and make it possible for you to grow crops? Do you feel gratitude for the person who plants the seeds and harvests the food? Do you feel gratitude for the transportation system that brings your food to where you live? Do you feel gratitude for the garbage man who picks up your trash, or the indoor plumbing in your house, or for the clean drinking water you have available? You are constantly supported every minute of the day by someone or something that helps you to live. You are never really alone or disconnected. When you are grateful for all that supports your physical and material life, you begin to see that you belong to something bigger than yourself. You see that the universe supports *all* that you are, not just your material existence. Then, joy begins to flow in you.

What is joy? Joy is a state of being. It effects and springs from the deepest parts of yourself. Joy is with you even when your goals are not achieved. Joy is the knowledge that you are *not* alone, that you are connected to everyone and everything, that you are part of the Divine Plan and deserve love and respect because you are part of the All. **Joy is being good enough**. Joy brings **contentment** with what is in you life and with who you are.

However, most of human behavior is based on seeking happiness, rather than joy. Happiness is of the material world and usually is achieved by setting and attaining goals. Because happiness is more associated with goals, it is temporary, limited and attached to a specific outcome or event and tends to evoke more desires. You can pursue one temporary thing after another and never experience a more complete satisfaction.

Wanting and achieving goals is not bad because this is how you grow and develop. As a child, you learn to walk and talk and go to school. Happiness results by achieving these milestones. As an adult, you get your first job, you first paycheck, and your first relationship. By wanting, setting goals and working to achieve these goals, you move forward in you life. Happiness can be the fulfillment of your material lives, but it does not completely satisfy you. You also need the joy that is connected to other more permanent aspects of yourselves.

You do need *both* joy and happiness. Joy and happiness balance the needs of both your material and spiritual natures and show that it is *both* realms that satisfy your deepest longings.

And so, gratitude is necessary because it keeps the flow of energy between you and the Divine open and moving. The fullness of life is experienced when both partners recognize their roles and act on them. How would *you* feel if you kept giving gifts that were not acknowledged or appreciated? Anyone, including the Divine, would stop the giving until the recipient was able to see and respond. So, gratitude seeds the ground to receive even more. The giver is happy to give when the recipient really sees the gift and responds. Gratitude opens the doors to receive. Then, joy comes up from being so supported. A lack of gratitude, on the other hand, stops the flow, and joy cannot be released.

Meditation for Wisdom-Key #8

Sit in your quiet place. Take slow, deep breaths. Remember all you have learned and all you now live. Call your Dragon to you. As your Dragon approaches, you bow to each other in acknowledgment of who are you. Your Dragon invites you to ride with him to a special destination. Climb aboard the Dragon's back and close your eyes.

When you feel the Dragon descend from your flight, open your eyes. Right below you sits the ancient ruins of a temple. Your Dragon lands in the field adjacent to the great stone floor that descends from the ancient altar. Gathered there are Dragons from many lands and places. They are all resplendent and jovial. You see them all standing side by side, forming a giant circle. As you land, they begin to pound their great feet in praise and celebration. You and your Dragon are admitted to the circle.

First you are asked to stand in the center. One by one, these great Masters bow to you to honor who you are and the life of integrity you have chosen. When the circle is finished, your Dragon steps forward and unravels an ancient scroll. Speaking clearly to all, your Dragon says: "Here I present the Dragon Master I have tutored. You, my special one, have chosen:

- To acknowledge the Divine Plan and your place in it
- To commit to this way of life
- To take action to fulfill your commitment
- To know that your discerning choices lead to abundance
- To experience lightness as a result of detachment
- To radiate compassion to all, including yourself
- And to experience gratitude and the joy that flows from it

Enter this circle now, the circle of those who serve the One and the Plan."

With that, you and your Dragon step back and are accepted into the circle. As the Dragons stamp their heavy feet on the earth, you join them in this dance of honor and acceptance and joy by stamping your feet as well. The earth seems to shake with the power of this declaration.

Then, the great Master Dragons begin to shoot fire from their mouths, fire that shoots upward in great balls of ignited power. These balls of fire shoot upwards and explode in colors, fireworks of joy and celebration. You watch the sky as starbursts of colored fire explode in geometric forms, even taking on the appearance of small burning Dragons. The sky is filled with color and with smoke as the celebration continues.

In the midst of all this, your Dragon leans close to your face and gently kisses you.

"Remember tonight, my sweet, even through the years ahead. Remember who you are. This can never be taken from you. **You are who you are** for all eternity."

When you are ready, you and your Dragon will return home. Stay in this reflective place for however long you desire.

Tools for Integration of Wisdom-Key #8

1. *Affirmations/Positive Self-Messages*—Repeat two times per day for two weeks:
   a. I am a being of light and joy.
   b. I radiate my joy to all those I encounter.
   c. My joy is based in the Truth and exists even in times of sadness.
   d. I can achieve experiences of happiness in my life without harming others.
   e. Joy and happiness are balanced in my life.
   f. I am grateful for all that I have and all that I am.
   g. I feel grateful for all that supports me.
2. *Journaling*—Take some quiet time and write from your own life experiences:

    a. What things brought happiness to your life in the past month? How long did this feeling last?

    b. When you are not actively pursuing a goal, what do you experience: contentment, upset, emptiness?

    c. Have there been times in your life when you have been hurt or treated unfairly or have done that to others in the pursuit of a goal? Explain.

    d. Do you measure your happiness by the amount of "stuff" in your life? If you don't possess the latest fad how do you feel?

    e. What makes you feel successful (career achievements, awards, recognition, salary, trips, doing good works)? Why?

    f. Write down all that supports you during one day of your life (e.g., the alarm clock that wakes you, the clean water you bathe with, those that make the soap and toothpaste you use etc.).

    g. What do you feel grateful for? Make a list.

    h. Is there joy in your life? What does that mean to you?

    i. As you observe others, can you recognize those that seem joy-filled, not just happy? What leads you to your conclusions?

3. *Other Activities*—These are different ways to integrate this Wisdom-Key:

    a. If you feel called to do so, make a gratitude altar for all that you have received from the Dragon teachers and others in your life.

Conclusion

What is different about this information?

Do the Wisdom-Keys help me to live in a new way?

Do the Wisdom-Keys give me a foundation on which I can build a meaningful and contributing life?

What is different about the Dragon Wisdom-Keys is that the Dragons give us the gift of recognizing and appreciating matter. The Dragons explain that matter is a co-equal partner with Spirit. The Dragons celebrate the body, matter and the Earth as Divine aspects and tell us that the body, matter and the Earth are not to be punished because they are sinful. The Dragons tells us that we cannot return Home without acknowledging and respecting this truth.

The illusions, that the Dragons help us to see clearly, create a toxic environment that we have absorbed. This toxic atmosphere tells us that matter is bad and sinful, that there is no plan for our lives, that we are all alone and in direct competition for everything, that resources are scarce and that we had better hang on tightly to everything that we have. The illusions tell us that commitment and action are *not* necessary and that compassion, sharing and joy are only believed in by fools. In short they tell us: *There is only One God and you are not It, and life goes downhill from there!*

These illusions, that we have grown up with and come to believe without even thinking, have caused us to believe in untruths that, in turn, have built a world that reflects the exact opposite of our Divine nature and of who we truly are. These illusions have led to a view of the world and of "human nature" that deforms our emotions, our thoughts and our bodies.

Let's look at an example involving children. We all know that if children are brought up in an environment that tells them they are stupid and bad that their lives can be permanently stunted. The children come to believe these lies and their self-confidence and self-esteem are damaged. They are not able to see themselves or others clearly. They are angry at themselves because they are not good enough and can never be. And, they are not at peace with themselves or others.

What happens when a room full or country full of children with low self-esteem and lots of anger is put together with others? There is violence, a pecking-order (class distinctions) is established, the physically strong or those that can manipulate others become leaders, and there is little room for love, compassion or justice. Those that are not in charge must follow or try to disappear from view and not make waves. Does this sound familiar in our world? Our world functions as it does because we all have accepted the illusions that the Dragons have been describing.

Let's exchange our illusions now for the truth, and our world will change into what we have only dreamed possible! Put the Dragon truths to work in your lives, and this change can begin immediately. One person at a time, one truth at a time is all it takes to begin a wonderful change on this planet!

The process of integrating Dragon wisdom into your lives, of seeing through illusions into truth, shakes up the cultural definition of reality, and there are consequences! Things will change, things will be released and new structures will be built. This can manifest in your bodies, in your emotions, in your thoughts, in your beliefs, in your relationships and life situations. When these changes occur, you will feel anxiety, but this is a sign that the process is working and that more changes are coming!

Because of the oneness of all reality, these changes not only impact your daily lives, but also affect your communities, countries, the world and the universe! This is not just an interior change of an individual, but change that will impact all creation. What effects one, affects all. "As above, so below and as below so above!"

We begin now to take our place as pioneers of a new world!

Appendix 1:Dragons and Feng Shui

In some schools of feng shui, Dragons are associated with compass directions and with the elements.

DRAGON OF THE NORTH
        337.5 degrees to 22.5 degrees
        Color : blues and black
        Element: water
        Number: 1

DRAGON OF THE SOUTH
        157.5 degrees to 202.5 degrees
        Color: red, rose, purple, yellow, bright orange
        Element: fire
        Number: 9

DRAGON OF THE EAST
        67.5 degrees to 112.5 degrees
        Color: greens and browns
        Element: wood
        Number: 3

DRAGON OF THE SOUTHEAST
        112.5 degrees to 157.5 degrees
        Color: greens and browns
        Element: wood
        Number: 4

DRAGON OF THE WEST

247.5 degrees to 292.5 degrees

Color: white, copper, gold, silver

Element: metal

Number: 7

DRAGON OF THE NORTHWEST

292.5 degrees to 337.5 degrees

Color: white, gold, silver, copper

Element: metal

Number: 6

DRAGON OF THE SOUTHWEST

202.5 degrees to 247.5 degrees

Color: brown, beige, terra cotta, dark yellow, dark orange, rust

Element: earth

Number: 2

DRAGON OF THE NORTHEAST

22.5 degrees to 67.5 degrees

Color: beige, brown, terra cotta, dark yellow, dark orange, rust

Element: earth

Number: 8

(This information from the Diamond School of Feng Shui)

Appendix 2: Ley Lines and the Dragons

The Earth herself, like all other parts of creation, is made of living energy. We see this same energy in ourselves. This life energy moves in a certain pattern of flow. We see the flow in our blood vessels, our nervous system and in the meridians used in acupuncture.

In the Earth herself, which is a much more complicated system, there are also energy patterns.

These energy patterns form a gigantic internal grid system in the Earth. Energies move through this system across the planet. In many traditions this grid is called "ley lines" or "Dragon lines". Dragons know about energy in matter and how this energy can best flow. In humans, if energy becomes stuck, sickness can result. In the Earth, a lack of flow can result in a deterioration of the entire ecosystem.

In Europe and Asia, the presence of Dragon-lines is talked about quite naturally. Many cathedrals of Europe have been built where ley or Dragon lines intersect because this is a powerful point of energy. We have called these intersections by various names: "vortexes" when they occur in the Earth and "chakra centers" when they occur in human energy fields.

Appendix 3: Kwan-Yin and Dragons

Kwan-Yin, the Chinese Goddess of Compassion, is a "Dragon-Rider." What does it mean to "ride the Dragon?"

To "ride" a Dragon implies the ability to direct our life energy with grace and ease.

Dragons, as we have seen, know a great deal about energy flow and about embodiment and balance. They are wisdom-keepers, able to see through the illusions of the world, knowing that, to be truly empowered, we must balance our material and spiritual natures. We must respect the natures of both matter and Spirit. Kwan -Yin and the Dragons appreciate human life and the difficulties we face. They ask us to value our humanity because it is our human experiences and sufferings that break open our hearts to allow Spirit to come *alive* in us. To truly value our humanity is to have compassion for all the cruelties, limitations and inadequacies we experience as we learn the necessary lessons that bring us home to the Divine.

So, Kwan-Yin is a being who is powerful because she has learned to balance the energy of Spirit and the energy of matter in this embodied world.

There are many legends about her. One legend says, in an earthly life, she gave *all* for the health of her father. She allowed her hands to be cut off and lost her vision to save him. She then was able to see beyond surface appearances, illusions or the personality. She saw with her heart, and was able to balance wisdom and compassion in herself so that she could share this with mankind.

So, we too are asked to become "Dragon-Riders", to balance the embodied life and the spiritual life, to see in deeper ways to penetrate the web of illusion and to live by truth.

Look for some depictions of Kwan-Yin riding a Dragon. Compassionate Mother, Kwan-Yin, knows that what the Dragons bring is valuable and helps us to become the powerful beings that we are as Children of the One.

Appendix 4: Meditation Practice

A consistent meditation practice is necessary to reshape your energy field by connecting with your "Higher Self". A constant practice also helps to clear your energy field and protect you. There are three aspects of the person: the personality/ego, the soul, and the Spirit/ I AM Presence. The personality/ego is made up of the physical body, the etheric body, the emotional body, and the mental body. The realm of the personality is where much of your "hang ups" and illusions of who you think you are, and the experiences of all lifetimes are stored. Until you clear the residue that is accumulated there, your energy will be stuck and not flow smoothly. A meditation practice can help you see where you are stuck and actively release the stuck energy.

A daily meditation practice is also important because, when you begin to work with your energy, it is important that proper boundaries be maintained.

These boundaries help you to distinguish your energy from the energy fields around you.

This also helps you to begin to protect your energy field.

Once the personality/ego begins to clear and you can distinguish your energy from others', the energy of your personality/ego can flow to and connect with your soul and Spirit/ I AM Presence.

If your practice does not include protection of your own energy field and connection to your soul and Spirit bodies, then you can insert this intention into your practice: to protect and clear your personality bodies and to connect to your soul and Spirit/I AM Presence/Highest Self.

1. There is a grand Plan for all creation, it includes you. }

2. Honor yourself & all creation

3. Commit next to the Truth ——→

4. The Principle of action is Needed for change to [accrue] ——

5. Abundance (through discerning choices) ——→

6. Non-Attachment & lightness ——→

7. Compassion (to feel together) ——→

8. Gratitude & joy (Keeps the flow between you & the Divine) ——→

Shift fundamental perspective ___

Aligning up
TRUE Self destiny blending Personality (Mature
    up I am presence (Spirit)

ID your goal · take action; Remain flexible
    Bring Spirit & form together though action

When you are balanced + aligned, abundance
    + grace.

Attachment = Nailed to; instead, Sly.

Judgment + Condemnation → Shortcomings → destruction →
Self-other hatred → Disrespect → Conflict + war
vs
Oneness in all creation
    Happiness = Seeking
             = getting + achieving there; temporary
             = material life
             = ground + desire of the Personality
        vs
    Joy = the Divine connection
        = Spiritual contentment

                Dragons
        Balance Energy   Master
            + Energy   Spirit

Personality (ego) ← Physical body
                    Etheric body
                    Emotional body
                    Mental body
Soul
Spirit (I am presence)

Boundaries

CPSIA information can be obtained
at www.ICGtesting.com
Printed in the USA
FSHW012238130121
77601FS